Journey to Chartres

Carolyn Grassi

❧

Journey to Chartres

Introduction by
LOUIS L. MARTZ

BLACK SWAN BOOKS

Acknowledgements are made to the following journals in which poems by
Carolyn Grassi have first appeared: *Brooklyn College Literary Review, Contact
II, The Owl, Passages North, San Jose Studies, Simone de Beavoir Studies,* and
Studia Mystica.

*for all those who believed in
and shared the journey . . .*

for Joseph, Edwin and Peter

New Poets Series 2

First Edition

Published by

BLACK SWAN BOOKS Ltd.
P. O. Box 327
Redding Ridge, CT 06876
U.S.A.

ISBN: 0-933806-55-8
LC Card: 88-8165

CONTENTS

II *Vision of Chartres*

III   *Gestures of the Word*

INTRODUCTION

AT A GLANCE, or even at a first casual reading, these poems may seem to be celebrating the culture of France. But a deeper, more sustained reading suggests that "France" is for this poet an immense and varied image of a region of the mind or soul in which the physical and the spiritual may live together in a fertile harmony. "France" becomes a mythic region toward which the poems long in memory and desire—a region where the poet can fulfill her womanhood and bring to birth the struggling muse that lives within her. This effect is enhanced by the interpolation of phrases, titles, and topics reminding us that the poems are being written in California. The "Journey to Chartres," then, is an interior journey in which memories of visits to France, reading in French writers, and seeing of works by French painters, sculptors, and architects form the ground from which the spiritual aspects of life arise, inseparable in this poet's imagination from the things of earth.

The sensory grip on life, especially the visual apprehension of earthly landscapes, whether in nature or in art, suggests a sensibility akin to that of Whitman, D. H. Lawrence, and William Carlos Williams. With Whitman she shares (perhaps with certain French poets as intermediaries—she quotes Saint-John Perse) the long flowing lines that evoke "the caresser of life, wherever moving." With Lawrence she shares the mysterious gift of sensing the "Strange storming up from the dense under-earth" of natural forces, "Setting supreme annunciation to the world," as in his "Almond Blossoms." And with Williams she shares the principle, "no ideas but in things"; she too seeks and finds "the Beautiful thing" that resides in affectionate human response. Like these poets, she celebrates the indestructible creative power that lives within the human consciousness.

She is a poet in the American grain, after the essential way described by Williams in his essay on Edgar Allan Poe, where he surprises his reader by choosing—not Whitman or Fenimore Cooper—but Poe as the example of one who is true to the "local"; Poe, who wrote of murders in the Rue Morgue and of strange happenings in houses that might be anywhere. Williams makes it plain, in what was meant to be the final, culminating essay of *In the American Grain*, that by "local" he does not mean simply American settings: Poe, he says, seeks "to find a way to tell his soul"—and so Poe attempts "to originate a style that does spring from the local conditions, not of trees and mountains, but of the 'soul'." "Poe could look at France, Spain, Greece, and *not* be impelled to copy. He could do this *because* he had the sense within him of a locality of his own, capable of cultivation."

A locality of her own: this is what these poems cultivate, as they move with grace, passion, and wit through the worldly works and scenes of France. The gardens of Versailles provide images of impassioned art, where statues and fountains flourish in one great animated design. By contrast, the grey palace of the popes at Avignon becomes an image of oppressive power, in which the poet's mind reverts to the writings of Balzac, with his love of the exact detail, the "vivid life underneath their music," and his deep insight into the motions of the desiring and suffering soul, which for Balzac, as for this poet, is imbedded in physical being. With "Balzac's words within" she finds her way down the "dark stairs" of the palace and out into the city's life—into Balzac's world:

> a young man strummed a guitar
> three children jumped beside the fountain
> a woman with brilliant black hair
> swayed on her lover's arm

Her meditation on novelists in "Three French Men" is in many ways a sure key to this poet's imagination. Stendhal, Proust, and Balzac are the favorites (significantly, *not* Flaubert: is he for her too limited, lacking in profound human sympathy?). These three, as the poet's caressing consciousness sweeps over them in something like a surrealist movement of collage, all share one essential quality: they love human existence, passionately, as they reveal in their extravagant affection for the details of human life. Stendhal, she says, "slept with every detail in his imagination"; Proust wrote "feminine embroidery in cascading sentences texturing sight / scent   taste"; Balzac "kept every draft of his letters / wanting to touch with words." Such is the world of the opening section: "Memory"—as we may see from the "cascading sentences" of "Music Room," "Provençal Summer," the sequence "Mont Saint Michel," or "Collaboration between the Sexes," the last being her poem on the relationship between Sartre and Simone de Beauvoir, where the journeys of the two through actual landscapes become explorations of the mind and soul in a companionship that offers a union of the best in man and woman.

One should not overlook the witty intellect that holds these vibrant materials under control. A poem such as "At the Louvre" begins with deliberate fragmentation and excited colloquial wandering, but then, as the image of the Mona Lisa (implied only) is at last discovered, the lines and language settle down into reverent and loving admiration: "she embraces all who stay / wanting a share in her wisdom." Her sympathetic and yet comic evocation of "Madame de Maintenon and the King's Love" works through ironical appreciation: "her generosity invited a heavenly reward." In a more somber tone the sharp, short lines of "Rouen: Joan of Arc's Trial by Absence" present the torments of doubt and defeat, in harsh contrast with the long lines that elsewhere so frequently celebrate the concrete appreciation of the earthly setting. Indeed, one might say that this constant intermingling of poems in flowing style with poems in short, abrupt lines (rather like H. D. in places) indicates the constant effort of the poet to rein in and guide the impulsive and almost overwhelming responses to nature and art that form the ground-tone of all these poems. One feels this tension (and the kinship with H. D.) very strongly in the ecstatic note of her firmly controlled poem on "The Niké of Samothrace":

> become   become the figure with foot raised
> over the water   stepping on to the shore
>
> be   be   the victory on the stairs
> turning on the inner axis of her resurrection

As the first section closes with the sequence on Mont Saint Michel, we are made to realize that religious feeling has never been absent in this early portion.

The poems on Chartres itself come in the second part, but it might be said that the looming vision of Chartres in the landscape is latent in the earlier journey through scenes that some, but not this poet, would call secular: her religious vision includes all. Thus the creative power seen in "The Rodin Museum" is a foreshadowing of the meaning of Chartres: "a final vision given weight / lifting enormous pieces into position"—"the Hand of God going over his original creation." And "The Cluny Manuscript," with its integration of sense and soul in the monkish painter, foreshadows the larger integration of Chartres. Again one thinks of Williams, with his admiration for the catholic sensibility of Père Sebastian Rasles, in that essay set in Paris, at the very center of his book, where Williams declares so fervently his allegiance to the view of life that he finds in the letters of Rasles: "Nothing shall be ignored. All shall be included. The world is parcel of the Church so that every leaf, every vein in every leaf, the throbbing of the temples is of that mysterious flower. Here is richness, here is color, here is form. . . . This is a moral source not reckoned with, peculiarly sensitive and daring in its close embrace of native things."

As we move into the "Vision of Chartres" the opening poem, "After the Queen," sets the theme of the need for the archetypal feminine: the vision of full womanhood developed in all the poems to the Virgin and her great manifestation in stone and glass; "she seems both chaste and sensual   the way of a woman with God"—"a woman ready to embrace life" in all its local movement and detail:

> you sit in the garden pavilion   overlooking the lake
> he leans back in your lap as your right hand lifts an Anjou pear
> he counts berries on a string   pages in the Book of Hours blow back
> sparrows sway on a rose bush   red-orange on white

> ("Notre Dame")

As the poems in chanting rhythm move through the stages of the ancient liturgy the poet recreates the meaning of the incantation in her own voice, the voice of a modern woman finding an answer to her need in the ancient archetype of human generosity and redemptive love of all creation. "Credo" says it all:

> I believe you are God's feminine country
> balancing rule with laughter   teaching with song
>
> *   *   *
>
> I believe you return as Eurydice to Orpheus
> not sinking back to the underworld
> but embracing Orpheus for daring to look
> for the courage to call her name
> to reach for her hand
> I believe you are the eternal woman

Yet the eternal woman is still "local." The fine poem on "The Birthing Garment at Chartres" opens with a tribute to the ancient relic, then moves in the second section to a naturalistic account of Christ's birth:

> . . . a panting breath
> pain absorbed as she grasps the sheets
>   bannering God's push forward
> through her labyrinth—*Lux aeterna*—
>   she wipes the blood from his face
> she opens the gauze round her breasts
>   his tiny mouth finds her food
> Paradise seems restored

Then, surprisingly, but deftly, the third section shifts to America:

> in California Charlotte weaves white cotton
>   a birthing garment   folded on a cream silk bed
> scarlet puffed gauze at the throat and entrance
>   every detail edged in delicate strength

And other women seem to create a sort of modern fertility festival:

> women   under a September moon in an adobe courtyard
>   Ilse plays the recorder   Jo Ann creates a chant
> Carol Lee   pregnant seven months—leads a belly dance
>   a nearby woman prays for a fertile womb

Then the final section returns to "Mary of Chartres," as she "slips the garment over her head":

> the organ releases   *"Alleluia Alleluia"*
>   *Regina Pacis   Regina Coeli   Regina Aeterna*
> her terra-cotta figure enthroned on the wall
>   scepter in hand   the infant comforted in her arms
> transparency folded in her foundation at Chartres

So then, the Queen has not died, after all; she lives, an intimate presence, abundant in all the epiphanies of this poet's vision.

The final brief section of the book may puzzle at first, but it seems to represent an envoy which tells of the struggle of the creative self to fulfill her vision of the world, tells of her frustrations and defeats, and also of her joy and delight in the discovery of the dance of words. "Gestures of the Word," the central poem here, seems to tell of the descent of poetical inspiration, "saying my name," creating "a landscape changed by language"—"igniting the earth under us   scorching / lines in the landscape   leaving an incision on the soul." It is always the soul. These closing poems reaffirm a religious unity: "Annunciation" here speaks of the birth of poetry.

But such epiphanies must have their shadows. The moving tale of the wounded doe "In the Forest" seems more closely akin to the surrealist fantasies of Magritte or Delvaux than to the painting by Franz Marc that provides its motive imagery. It tells perhaps a personal story; but the meaning is universal: the rejection of essential femininity by the outer (male) consciousness which (as with Emily Dickinson) does not understand the strange intensity of utterance and moves abruptly and uncomfortably away. But the wound is not fatal: she would

> coax back her art with gentle words
> resurrect the gardens of France
>
> She will read beloved authors
> resay their words in her heart
> she wants more than survival
> she wants to sing again

And so, in the next poem, "With the Oil of Myself," she anoints the muse within, and before long she feels

> elusive cadences rise
> out of nothingness
> they take a human form
> and wish clothing for words

It was bound to be a difficult journey, beginning again and again. Thus the first poem in this "envoy" is appropriately entitled "Advent," the perpetual renewal of all creation in a dark season:

> it is necessary
> for the poppies
> to dip underground in shadow
> if to rise as flamed tongues in summer
>
> come   said the angel
> come   store the sap
> and learn how the invisible
> works without worry
>
> each month his nearness
> shapes the enfolded secret
> under her heart
> the ripening Word

And the last poem of the book is appropriately "Thérèse of Lisieux," who here becomes not so much a saint as a poet who realizes the essential union of body and soul:

> you came with his words in your hands
> the pages blazed between the cover
> vulnerable in their loveliness
> you touched his essence as you read
> God lived secretly in sounds

—Louis L. Martz

I *Memory*

So It Seems Possible in Paris in Summer

it is summer again along the boulevards
where the cafés are shaded yellow   white   blue   bronze
with canopied umbrellas over small oval tables
where white and red wine flow and beer foams

the air is heavy with mid-August heat
in the Luxembourg Gardens grandparents oversee
the children sailing boats and riding tricycles
while modern couples relax with the Sunday papers

as a man in a striped pastel shirt
encircles the waist of a woman dressed in white linen
as they listen to outdoor music from a small band
near bunches of red   yellow   pink   flower beds

even now in California   I remember the dust
swept high by straw brooms under oaks and plane leaves
in the Tuileries where an old woman sits on a bench sunning
near a young mother who shows off her beautiful baby

while Renoir swings a cane as he strolls
singing under his breath of pink flesh
and tinted cheeks   rounded hips   a fine bosom
and how to make it happen on canvas

while Toulouse-Lautrec mutters
how the chorus girls keep him busy at night
how the light of day hurts his eyes
how he loses perspective in broad daylight in the park

and Monet makes miniature loops with his fingers
unconsciously as he converses with a woman
as if drawing a rare flower that leads him
into coloring   shade and the indices of its heart

while Bonnard jokes about parrots in the morning
jumping out of Parisian windows   landing on men's heads
not on their hats   since one hardly ever wears a hat
the birds making a mess in white as a woman in blue watches

Simone de Beauvoir extols the graces of the intellect
harmonized with the peculiar situation of woman
wishing for each the mastery of self
she rushes ahead while many try to catch up

she turns toward Stendhal who steps from a bookstore
giving a wink   meaning "I've met my match in you"
he tips his hat   she acknowledges with a nod
they stroll off together and their talk is charged with sparks

so it seems possible   in Paris   in summer

If You Had Come to Paris

if you had come to Paris
we'd stand on the shaded stone of Sainte Chapelle
where Saint Louis walked barefoot to the pulpit
within the royal blue and gold sanctuary
we'd browse in book stalls along the Seine
rest in the garden of Notre Dame contemplating her buttresses
we'd shop the Galleries Lafayette for earrings and perfume
sit at an outdoor café commenting on the men and women passing
we'd attend Mona Lisa's afternoon audience at the Louvre
stroll before Queen Marie de Médicis in her gallery
we'd have Gruyère cheese   fresh bread   *vin blanc* in the Tuileries
watch the children sailing ships in the basin under plane trees
we'd dodge oncoming cars at the Place de la Concorde
run under green Neptune's mist as he sprays the nymphs
we'd head up the Champs Elysées browsing for records and books
take in a French film or an American with sub-titles
we'd walk arm in arm through the Arc de Triomphe
glancing back at the Louvre   a château in the distance
we'd visit the Paris Foreign Mission Society
a quiet refuge that continually sends young men to foreign lands
round the corner from Rodin's studio where you'd hold my hand
near Adam and Eve   Eros and Psyche   Orpheus and Eurydice
we'd return through the Faubourg Saint-Germain   where Proust
frequented salons of women who resembled rare birds
in gestures   manners   speech   scent   color   pleasuring his pages
for a further intimacy   when at home with pen in hand
as now I offer a few details so next time you'll come

Marie Antoinette at Saint Cloud

the sun on the stairs   shimmers
the chateau mirrors light off the Seine
the red damask room remembers
the rendezvous   the caress   the farewell
the blue marble star fading
where once in its center hope blazed
over the roses whose stems carry memory's blood
only a cut in the land   now   after the war

she waited for him through that first winter
trusting the bare arms of elm and maple
she was a water lily twisting under December clouds
lifting her face to January's harshness
under lamp light she strolled the garden
undressed alone before the evening fire
standing before the mirror wanting him

she touched the frosted grass   their shields melted
tiny shoots of Easter pushed under her palm
she let her hair grow longer

in August she heard his steps on the stairs
she rushed out   wanting to release
what she held all year
multiple sounds swarmed her breast   an intimate Pentecost
the statues at the entrance watched in contentment
their lips a vivid pink   supple under the sun's pressure
dolphins bore fiery water songs
the nymph responded to Neptune's advances

The Lilies *of Claude Monet*

(The Orangerie, Paris)

yellow desired blue   ivory wanted
purple   lavender rested in white
olive green shaded pink

as a young man touched a woman's
dark hair   at the train station
her intonation colored his afterwards

then Rouen's lace spilled on the floor
her stained roses splintered
her grief as if abandoned by God

a white line set off her figure
through her torn side   the violet sky
nights bronzed by a fiery memory

finally he coaxed the pale buds
on the morning pond   caressing the foliage
as she relaxed   unbuttoning her dress

after desertion   and   desolation
a tender contemplation of wounds
the soothing of scars   the erasing of indifference

tight fears eased in the August sun
trust grew textured and intimate
as a sanctuary of lilies

the Easter candle   incandescent at night
affinity   brilliant on the canvas
petaled wings resurrected

Strasbourg's Palace

the morning air   blond and balmy in August
    cobblestones   a small garden square
dazzling red   emphatic white   royal blue
    linden trees quiver in yellow-green flashes
the sun absorbs the stone façade of the basilica
    as a porous fabric soaks up liquid

now morning off high windows is crimson sheeted
    penetrating   red velvet drapes
over damask flowered chairs   resting
    as a pulse on the parquet floor
out of reach   not out of sight
    of the distant aching mirrors
desire swells in brightness
    glorious in crystal chandeliers

while in a private alcove a woman waits
    her brown eyes alive with light
her swan-white skin tinged by pink
    her hair cascades under a blue scarf
her full lips slightly open   as if in prayer
    her forest-green dress caresses her figure
around her neck a gold medallion
    her left hand fully open on her breast
she looks to her right   into the next room
    startled by the man's grey-blue eyes
his full lips   tender and intelligent
    how broad his forehead and strong his hands

he wears an amber shirt and brown pants
      he stands as if about to stride
a miniature Book of Hours in his left hand
      his right resting on his thigh as he moves
near the woman whose hand is on her breast
      as an offering   a promise   a tease

all afternoon she follows the sun on his figure
      in his subdued silence   she longs for
his footsteps at night   to touch his shoulders
      her face in his neck   her lips on his ear

now he thinks he knows secrets of the universe
      and she something of the sun's origin
tomorrow his hands will be restless as he watches
      from the next room how the light goes over her
as the drapes in large windows are caressed by silk cords
      as the mirrors quiver in their frames
as she remembers the suggestion of his form

The Rodin Museum

(Hôtel Biron, Paris)

noises of chisels chipping marble and clay
polishing   sanding   begetting details
of nose   eyes   ears   small bones   veins   hips
a final vision given weight
lifting enormous pieces into position

the hôtel's every room with Rodin's work
as if he left for a vacation and will soon return
each piece turns in slow motion as he set it
the muse hovers over the poet's head as he listens
Cupid holds Psyche's breast as they embrace in air
about to part   but never separating

Eve crouched into herself
absorbing a great grief
she protects her privacy
Adam is tortured by the forever possible
what might have been   haunts his shadow

light illumines the huge chest of Balzac
the open mouth of John the Baptist
the forehead of Victor Hugo
the two hands holding a secret in their palms
the Hand of God going over his original creation
as traffic hums over the wall near Les Invalides

The Cluny Manuscript

(Musée de Cluny, Paris)

the Cluny manuscript of the Middle Ages in my hands
thick brown leather   gold edged   enclosed in glass
opening on to a grey château in the days of Roland
a cathedral spire overlooking a town square
where Jeanne d'Arc dismounted to crown the King of France

the paint is drying on the September scene
a thick burgundy   moss green   royal blue
men in rust shirts carry burlap bags heavy with grapes
women in white bodiced blue dresses bend to fill the bags
their hands high overhead or touch their breast as in prayer

while in the monastery library   the warmth of candles
parchment in a monk's hands as he falls in love with the woman he paints
she presses grapes   nurses her child   lays food on an outdoor table
at night he dreams he is holding her in his arms
breathless by morning   he makes his way after Mass to his desk
brush in hand   he touches her hair   her face   her hips   her breasts

I also caress these Cluny pages with gold and blue lettering
as if silk threads in the Unicorn tapestry in the nearby rotunda
or as Sainte Chapelle's stained glass in tiny frames in the hallway
blues of strong respect   red wines of desire   blond purity preserved
in this harvest scene made beautiful by a monk's hands

while downstairs Roman baths flood with light from enormous windows
near an alcove where an abandoned altar clasps the sun to its heart
a bell rings   a taper rises to white wax
a rose in the courtyard wavers in the wind
a monk bows his head in prayer   in desire   in painting

At the Louvre

detoured by The Three Graces   The Winged Victory of Samothrace
the Venus de Milo   I snap their photo   no flashes allowed

these ladies leave off interviews   seem to say
—I am what I am—you get what you see—
                                        (grace   form   ecstasy)

where is she   I roam rooms of Greek and French art
it's hot   no air conditioning   the tourists thick

I can't figure out the floor plan
finally   a large Italian room on the right

a huge crowd is pressed to the side   against a glass case
a young woman sits on top a young man's shoulders

cameras click   a guard shouts—no flashes   no flashes—
how will I make it to the front   no one is moving

I push in   weave slowly forward
finally I find her holding court

I want to offer candles   incense   flowers
I have her in focus   will the film work without a flash

she is content   nonchalant   undisturbed by thousands
how well proportioned   stately   accessible   private

her hands just below her bosom   her glowing golden skin
laughing eyes   a penetrating   enigmatic smile

about to say something   deciding on silence
how a woman appears after making love

how she holds her body after prayer
how in repose after kissing her child goodnight

she embraces all who stay
wanting a share in her wisdom

The Niké of Samothrace

I will grow from my shoulders
wings that catch the morning light

I will stand on the prow of the ship
listening for water touching land

I will raise my arm and wave to you on the shore
and you will wear a diadem glowing on your brow

—come   come   the body ripens the soul
and the fruit of Life's tree is delightful

taste   taste the liquid songs of summer fountains
of man's return home to the Mediterranean basin

love   love on the carpet of a nearby forest
doves   cannot restrain their pleasure

wings   wings on the shoulders
she is more earthly than angels

absorb   absorb the light through an open window
alive in silence   two hearts correspond

become   become the figure with foot raised
over the water   stepping on to the shore

be   be   the Victory on the stairs
turning on the inner axis of her resurrection—

Madame de Maintenon and the King's Love

". . . it is proof of deep inferiority in a man if he cannot make his wife his mistress. Seeking variety is a sign of impotence. Constancy will always be the guardian spirit of love, evidence of immense creative vigor. . . . A man must be able to find all women in his wife. . . ."

Cousin Bette by Balzac

I

Louis loved the four nymphs alongside Neptune at Versailles
as they uncovered their breasts   removed his clothes
poured water over his hands and feet
combed his hair   perfumed his body with roses

II

they say the King sowed "his oats" in several women
his Spanish wife Maria-Theresa knew
who supplanted her   the Marquise Montespan
a fresh guide in the bed chamber
until a matronly tutor for the children arrived
a mature woman to shape the king's confidence
while the convent closed in on the Marquise

III

Madame de Maintenon won as a religious lover
she wooed with black satin
gold appliqué   a full bust   wide hips
a white laced-silver bordered mantilla
a long chain round her ivory neck
a plain gold cross above her cleavage
a Book of Hours clasped over her heart

IV

how she cared for Louis' soul through her body
what education   discipline   prayer   advice   duties read aloud
she kept religion lively in a maternal sensual breast
she handled state affairs as his equal
they wed secretly   the king offered a suite of rooms
a magnificent château over a lake outside Paris

their intimacy began each day   several times a day
causing Madame to complain to her confessor
who consoled her   insisting she kept the king from sin
her generosity invited a heavenly reward

V

Louis enjoyed Apollo's basin below his bedroom window
a wide canal before a background of poplars
a golden chariot drawn by dolphins   a muscular golden god
who worked heaven as earth wooed him closer   closer
a soothing goddess helped his hesitation home

Rouen: Joan of Arc's Trial by Absence

". . . sorrow is like the iron prop sculptors place
inside a clay figure, it is supporting, it is power."

Béatrix by Balzac

afterwards you gazed
through a tiny hole
in the thick tower   you knew
they carried wood for your pyre

at that moment did you tremble
did you doubt the future
were you crushed by their indifference
did you promise God
you would follow the call
if there was a beginning over

I am asking if you doubted at the end
as your work found no sympathetic ear
as your body was stripped of protection
as the soul you offered
was being smothered

your cry goes through me
every chamber trembles
the tiny veins in my throat
vibrate with grief

this is the turning point
when the voices stay silent
when the self is in ashes

you are an abandoned woman
in the middle of Rouen
within sight of the laced cathedral
you defend your voices with silence
as the name fool is thrown at you
as they say   your life is wasted

in these bitter moments
I taste defeat
I cry with you for God
and experience his absence
without a care-taker
without a witness
what is the future

will he come
will he come
I call his name
as the flames lick my breast
I feel his shape about me
as a Phoenix rising

Reims Cathedral

after the train   we head north-east up the hill
towards her towers   her façade and luminous plaza
where provincial women sell home-made lace at small tables
where Joan of Arc dismounted to crown the King of France
where an archangel stands smiling by the door
where Notre Dame de Reims watches with the sun in her face
angels running round her portal
while inside her story brocaded in silk
her birth   annunciation   coronation
her body   secretly conceiving God's sweet seed

we drink champagne at a nearby café
before the pleasure of her graceful arches
the hint of rose color in her cheeks
as she sits on her chair
God at home on her lap
such effervescent prayer
heady bubbles under hot skin
rising through our body
to the top of our head

Boulevard St.-Germain

arrows artfully aimed   a man's glance
appreciating his target

heat on my neck   in my breast
I stroll slowly   sway my hips slightly

a new way of walking   he's watching
my high heel catches in a grate near his table

inviting dark eyes and playful
a relaxed   intimate expression

my cheeks   hot to my fingers
his glance caresses without embarrassment

the next day I wear a white cotton sheath dress
gold earrings   a necklace   no bra   an extra bounce in my walk

Music Room at Santa Clara and Trianon

sister in the garden   where berries are heavy in the colors of Fall
and in your body the juices impatient   under the breath's tempo
so it's impossible to ignore the late afternoon piano music
reminding me of ballet classes when I was a child
as you easily open one arm   wide   followed by the other
music thickening the air with grace   intelligence   charm   realizing
from signs in Nature   such beauty's transient   fading at the finger-tips
so I promise to etch your features in poems on paper
allowing me comparison with the peony's temperament
in the defiant brightness young girls give
in the sound of silk   apparent in arabesques
suggested by the rustle of cotton   organza   satin   linen
as the imagination dances in the fragile   substantial embrace
roses give   without calling attention to themselves
leaving us free   as you   without confessions to offer
no diaries on the shelf   no poems with your signature
innocent of ambition   you bleed from harsh words   cold glances
burning incandescent at night for one man
as your green terraces carve a forest of pines and poplars
violets hide on the path's edge before pink begonias
in your eyes flashes of amber dance on blue
as the sun touches the pavilion's pink marble star
drawn to its topaz center as lilies rise white and yellow from water
swans push off in paired sequences from the shore
gold embraces pine-wood in raised roses   bluebirds   grapes   pears
trees by the door taste in their roots   spring's water

The Kiwi Torte

(Pâtisserie, Rue du Parchemin, Strasbourg)

the lime kiwi with dark flecked freckles
blond hair spiralled round her
relaxing on the bed of a tan floured torte
wearing her heart exposed   wanting to be tasted and known
to be remembered   not only for her fine flavor   slightly tart
but for her crystal covered sweet glazed gown
that domesticates her island freedom
into a proper place on the glass shelf of Grauffel's bakery
beside the traditional apple and restrained pear
whose appearances also are lovely   transparent and glowing
elegant for the eyes   inviting for the tongue

as how certain women want their appearance as enough for a man's eyes
yet feel their emotions leaning into their figure   dress   manners   speech
as if their clothes were only containers for something better
beneath the wrapper   promising taste   enjoyment and more
offering a fine fruit   enjoyed best when taken home to bed
similar to the kiwi   apple   pear   whose green   red   or pale blond color
shape   size   texture   taste is best discovered in leisure
intensified by a fine restaurant   linen napkins   wine   a secluded table
as with special ways of making love on a vacation in France
flowered curtains   the red fleurs-de-lis wall-paper   white percale sheets
the bedding making her body more beautiful as if she lounges in a fancy bakery

By the Church Door, St.-Germain-des-Prés

> *"What I have loved most in life . . . have been its reveries."*
> —Stendhal

an elderly woman with long white hair tied in a bun
eyes cast down   sits straight against the back-wall
her black dog sleeping by her side
her graceful hand lifted   without looking up   *"Merci, Madame"*

did she love and give love   did she know better days
her good looks evident in a black velvet dress
her laughter   her subtle charm   her quick wit
so men found her irresistible   competing for her attention

now in her last years   cast off
adrift in a gorgeous city   making do
with train stations   church doors   rest rooms costing a franc
though   she remains regal   attractive   secretive

not without what went before
when her body made light of its beauty
generous   giving   enjoying what others enjoyed of her
now   silence surrounds her reveries

France and Suburban California

this street in northern California's named White
for its double lined birches that nearly kiss in the middle
as beautiful as the Versailles forests
laid out by Louis XIV in patterned flowered paths

here at the intersection near Benton
a bush blooms in mid January with pink profusion
full   languorous   generously scented
you'd think the month was June

in the Luxembourg Gardens
the senses intoxicated by naked pink buds
swaying at a distance but near enough to tempt
the white bark's maturity to burst

out with the yellow-green hair of Spring
now a chaste glance   now strong legs quiver
as the brave bosomed rose refuses pruning
offering the pleasure of her final perfume

As in a French Painting

". . . for Monet or Corot . . . will do our loving for
us. Then we shall love. . . . But on the threshold of
love we are bashful. There has to be someone who
will say to us, 'Here is what you may love; love it.'
And then we love."

—Marcel Proust

a mirror   according to light or shadow
darkens or clarifies the image
giving off an unbiased reflection
not always with a painting

imagine a dancer by Degas   a courtesan by Renoir
a 14th century Madonna   a mother by Raphael
is she old fashioned   lovely   shy   intelligent
is she remote   elusive   accessible   inviting

the woman's profile in the garden window
a moment of introspection
she wears a deep green dress
her hair is curled   her lips rosed

through open louvre doors we hear
birds   lovers   water   the wind
we touch summer humidity on her skin
Degas' intensity's involved

what of the woman in Bonnard's painting
washing in the bathtub upstairs near the window
her long hair golden in the sun
light caresses her shoulders

Bonnard's glances give her a start
he cares for how she touches her breasts
as she bends over and washes with suds
—please keep the cotton cloth slightly on—

what of the 14th century Madonna in the Cluny monastery
interested in secrets of the universe
God asks for a home in her womb
his tiny hands pull at her neck   grab her hair

or is she a man's psyche
as he paints her in that intimate moment

The Priest at the Madeleine

it is how devotion   over a life-time   shapes the body
this priest after Mass shuffles through the side door
turns toward the altar   bows his head as he genuflects
crosses himself   assists some children

suffering and loneliness have subdued youth and vigor
his shoulders are bent from people's problems
how the best of women are betrayed and he cannot prevent it
how some die young   how others lose their jobs

he dresses plainly as if a simple shop keeper
his eyes reflect the candles from his favorite altar
he whispers to the Virgin as when a shy young man
renewing his vow to serve others   asking her help

he reminds me of Balzac's Abbé in *Ursule Mirouet*
content with "whist" at a friend's on Saturday nights
generous with compassion   not stingy with praise
he blushes at honors   lowers his head   makes a joke

his pleasure is listening to Mozart
on a summer afternoon   played by a beautiful woman
he is moved to tears by da Vinci's Madonna at the Louvre
his habit is tea in the Rodin garden after touring the museum

I ask prayers for my sons   who travel home alone to America
he wants the exact date of their departure
he promises: "I will be sure to remember them"
shaking my hand he says: "Enjoy your vacation in Paris, Madame"

Three French Men

Stendhal makes me weep   his continual disappointment   his obsession for
the Italian countess Matilde as fierce as Dante for Beatrice   the same
seeing her on the street   his legs weakened   he needed to
support himself against a wall   he was excessive when speaking with her
sounding stupid   or restrained   only a few words   or he stayed silent
seeming stupid   she offered two visits a month   he circled the calendar
anticipating the nights in her parlor   sweating on his way   trembling
as he rang the bell   knowing he was one man among many others   desperate
for the smallest affection   often ignored   even so in *Love* Stendhal
painted woman as noble   more kind than petty   more tender than proud
generous even in refusals   he favored her   features as a da Vinci
Madonna   a new Eve   he slept with every detail in his imagination
touching her tender parts   pretending she lived only for him
he held her close   her every word   gesture   expression   believing
at the next visit   she would shower undivided attention on him

Proust enchants me with long paragraphs of flowers   feelings   family
an aristocrat   an impressionable child   a flamboyant man   a modern
artist   feminine embroidery in cascading sentences   texturing sight
scent   taste   a boy with his mother bending over his bed
a mature man's impeccable form as he folds the past in the present
a multi-colored symphony   tense   teasing   holding   releasing a beautiful
painful ether as when he hides outside a woman's home watching her
silhouette as she undresses   worrying if someone's arm is round her
if the shadows conceal a rival   the torment lasting over a hundred pages
he needed to know where she was   draw near her perfumed flesh
see the silver bracelet heavy on her wrist   the diamond on her breast
beside a bead of sweat   he scented her bed at night with hawthorn and lilac
he was beside her at a dinner party   noticing a handsome Count's conversation

refined manners of a Duchess   or cutting remarks of a self-centered host
was Proust an eternal *puer*   boy of his mother's bosom   waiting in bed
for morning conversation   tea   the newspaper   and pleasant weather

Balzac as intimate and overwhelming   larger than life   as the bust Rodin
shaped   his dream of being a Bonaparte in literature   everything shaped
for that effect   he created a "Human Comedy"   man as miser   minister
printer   father   writer   pretender   lover   woman as mother   courtesan
daughter   countess   wife   virgin   painting Parisian and provincial parlors
where avarice rivaled love in passion   so a man's sex fired his brain
or a woman's ambition as a heart of steel   her eyes glacial blue   or
a woman's dark eyes drawing a man with the warmth of her soul as Eve
won Balzac with her letters after reading his novels   she was overcome
on her couch   worrying her family   correspondence begun in a newspaper
Balzac daring as a boy   confident as a man   meeting Eve by a Swiss lake
she wore a violet dress   they knew each other immediately in the crowd
though they never met before   for eighteen years he waited   finally she
married him just before he died   he needed her body and soul
she entered his writings   her passions   faults   darkness   desires
understanding their source   needing Eve as his haven   sweet scent
rewarding his labor   he kept every draft of his letters
wanting to touch with words   draw her within his novels   hold her close

Rodin in the Afternoon

(Stanford University)

more than anything else in Rodin's room   I notice woman's form
floating   firm   focused   who I am   and am becoming

marble   limitation   reserved   steady   strong
terra-cotta clay   impressionable   pliable   surrendering

my psyche   my muse   myself
center of folds   turning currents of contemplation

twin women embrace in a dance of clouds   drift together
electricity magnetizes their bodies   form offers freedom

a man and woman touch in a flash of separation
a goodbye kiss   held   in their gesture the look of return

the unseen sex   secretly couched in two hands
the cathedral rising from arched fingers

a single touch of meditation on my breast
same as the woman stepping from the bath drying her hair

as if Rodin's strong hands and powerful palms
made the most delicate details of a woman's body live

Psyche's wings rise from female flesh
Eros embraces her contours   seeks her soul

such smiles on the lovers' faces
noticed in the small lines near their eyes

The Children's Fate

(Rue des Deux Ponts, Île St. Louis, Paris)

the long slender flamed lily from mounds of pink begonia
violets and mums on the silk lawn at Jardin des Plantes
where Rilke walked as a young poet
where a grandmother in a cotton pink dress
pushes her grand-daughter's stroller
while three gardeners chat as they clip hedges
while another sweeps the park path with a straw broom

the child and grandmother's elegant apartment on the Île Saint Louis
boxes of chartreuse ferns on the ledge overlooking a courtyard
glazed peaches in tan fluted crust on the kitchen table
gold summer nights behind Notre Dame
her full buttresses   ancient flanks   rose brooch windows
city sights on either side of the Seine   the bells of the hour
the grandmother's kiss   her warm embrace outlined in the open window

years later   a brass plaque on the apartment façade:
"In 1942 children were taken from here to concentration camps"

the grandmother sleeps in earth
the child   before her time   dreams how it used to be . . .

Palais des Papes, Avignon

"O frontier, O silence! Aversion of the god!"
—Saint-John Perse

I entered the Popes' Palace at Avignon
guarded by soldiers with swords against me
I wore a magic cloak and passed unnoticed
up white granite steps of an inner court
under a heavy grey tower raised as a fist
in the sky   warning all who passed within

an enormous dining hall   a colossal ceiling
three stories tall in burnished rafters
two long tables ruled by princes of the church
whose center-piece a Papal throne in brocaded silk

cold air brushed my cheeks
empty of the Virgin   Magdalene or Anne
the bedchamber painted with geometrics   stags   dogs
pheasants   dark leaves   swords   and   thin fruits

Balzac portrayed his lover's home in Tours
a meadow of poppies and a walnut grove
yellow-white violets in a semi-circle round a pond
high dormer windows over double oak doors
her insignia carved *"Amitié"* in gold-leaf

intimacy hinted at in words
a glove on her hand
a fabric shaded   enveloping her figure
his soul breathing her near   intelligent   fragrant
glances   disguises   jokes   innuendos   retreats

a vivid life underneath their music
stars   birds   flowers   a river   a horizon lively with poplars
she set blue and gold dishes on the table   he fingered
her heavy red drapes   offset by a cream cotton valance
he opened his shirt   relaxed   in a tapestried chair
her signature sewn discreetly   hers alone

Balzac's words within as I walked the fortress
through a wide empty hall as high windows released
a harsh light without shadows or alcoves of privacy
all focused at the front for a raised throne

I found my way through the guards' room
down dark stairs until Avignon's square
a young man strummed a guitar
three children jumped beside the fountain
a woman with brilliant black hair
swayed on her lover's arm

Sculptures in the Gardens at Versailles

I

were they asked to pose
    to stay behind
    as figures of art. . . .

II MORNING

she kneels with a shell in her hand
    scooping the morning sun off the water
her back curved forward   she draws the liquid
    a posture rarely taken by a man
a slim ribbon between her breasts
    over her shoulder   down her back
to twin dimples of the hips

III AIR

another woman shades her face
    with a veil billowing air
as she eyes the horizon
    searching the chateau windows
        —where has he gone—
        —where is he waiting—
        —when will I follow—
has she agreed to remain
    nude to the waist
as other women in the garden

IV BACCHUS

nearby Bacchus feigns friendship
    keeper of the harvest
muscular   arms   legs   chest
    giving his strength tenderness
he risks ridicule with laughter
    a fig leaf fails to hide his beauty
he offers his form for the artist
    lips and brow detail yes
his legs assure commitment
    intimacy in the hands
pleasurable harvest and mouth
    his breathing warms the air
his glance goes to the woman
    who scoops up water or is it
for the one who shades her eyes

V DIANA

Diana deep in the forest
    keen eyes   exquisite hearing
surprised at the sound of another
    pursued as the prize
surveyed as a stranger
    she draws arrow to bow
spins on her toes   legs firmly apart
    tension in her breast
she sighs   sighting his figure
    her body quivers
she fears losing her balance
    she stretches the bow

her arms are aching
     she eyes the target
holding him in sight
     hesitant in letting go
swish . . . the arrow races
     she concentrates
he calls   Diana   Diana
     she feels her flesh cut
this wound of Cupid's

     VI THE WOMAN
the woman
in Neptune's fountain
offering and dreaming
unclothed   relaxed
lips   firm   tranquil
translucent eyes shaded
secret sensitive ears
her bronze figure greened
through several centuries
she waits for his advance
each gesture held
in anticipation
her left leg lifted
bent at the knee
her sceptre casual
on the side
near her foot
as her toes
touch the basin

This Island of August: Versailles

I wish for the temperature of August
again along the northeastern path
that is shaded by a thick pine forest
opening as a circle by the Summer fountain
where a woman reclines on a bed of wheat
while naked children play round her legs

I see the cleavage of white clouds
I hear the gathering birds
in deep green shadows on the wing
near my feet as I undress my hair
I lift the flowers to my breast
I bear blond stalks in my arms
toward the radiant figure of Apollo
who wears the sun in his brow   whose voice
eyes   shoulders   hips magnetize
as dolphins in curved surrender
swim near his chariot

we gaze at each other's circle
surrounded by a calmly devoted nature
water lifts from sleep   pouring as
sheaves of ripened wheat
a fine laced spray
a liquid musical film
a mist falling in rivulets
over shoulders   arms   breasts

I am subdued by Summer's touch
I sing   am under his spell
the seasons of Autumn and Winter
whose signature fans toward me
from the quartet of paths
in scarlet flickering light I rest
I remain in this refuge
for the rhythm   the renewal
of swelling   sweet Summer
in the circular island of August

38

Fontainebleau—Memory

I remember your profile on the horizon
along the green slope   by poplars as you rode
near the silver-green fish that cleaved clearly near the wall
the oak leaves swayed   the wind echoed your name
attuned to my need as I waited on the white stairs
in the virginity of your absence   I imagined how
you might take me at the forest's core   fingers interlaced
touching seven streams   as they galloped in a wide lake
an island   fish   swans   birds   water lilies and rowboats
sweat and sweetness coupled in elm and pine
rose and begonia   shimmering waters circled
lifting a fountain   desire freshly formed
free   and   hopeful   at last   the restless day
attained an intimate form   as serene
as clear   as silent   as pulsed as water
as devoted   as close   as surprised   as a fountain
we sipped each other's color   longed for each other's fragrance
our language whispered   caressed   laughed   dared act foolish
tender   romantic   as Neptune sporting the nymph in his bronze arms
hidden springs rushed through chambers   passageways
the queen applauded   without fear   loss   or   regret
swans descended   stayed   lifted along the canal

Mother and Son (I)

(Mme. Jeanne Weil Proust 1849–1905, Marcel Proust 1871–1922)

the paths in Père Lachaise weave under numerous plane trees
your name in gold letters on black near your mother

pink and mauve roses   orange white gladiolus
placed by a woman's hand   on the black marble surface

how long ago that separation   your heart breaking
she was your hawthorn   perfume   humor

she carried your failures   healed them in her bosom
she celebrated your successes   promising a glorious future

her goodnight kiss   a benediction throughout childhood
her morning voice   a song—"Now, how is my lamb today?"

the scent of her embrace   tender   reassuring
her blue-black hair beside your face

her steps sounding on the stairs   her hesitation at your door
her entering on tip-toe   afraid she might wake you

she needed to know if your asthma kept you awake
she touched your cheeks and forehead   her hand in your hand

your face on her breast   warmth and safety   her arms rocked you
at a dinner party   electricity in her eyes   their transparent kindness

your names near   a closeness   gravitating souls
Père Lachaise as home   fragrant roses   brilliant gladiolus

Mother and Son (II)

(after reading conversations between Proust and his mother)

it is not possible to forget how it was
as I looked in the mirror at my body

I touched my curves   saying this is my fruit
how ready I was for your coming

for nine months how heavy and alive my middle
I circled the due date for June or July   I ate healthy food

your father said he'll never forget my radiant face
as he visited me in the hospital the night I delivered

how express those moments
when I offered my breast the first time

when tiny lips pulled for nourishment
when my womb contracted in contentment

routine was suspended for days
you wanted to nurse when I least expected it

I laughed as you played with a rubber giraffe in your mouth
kicking your legs in excitement at a magic lantern over your crib

I held you in my lap   face to face   we spoke
noises that made no sense to anyone else

you tried high notes reaching for words
you laughed at the songs I sang from my childhood

at four months you pulled yourself up by my fingers
you stood on my thighs

at eleven months in your first steps
you climbed the hill in front of the house

I pushed your carriage in every kind of weather
the blue sky of your eyes   the sun on your lashes

your small arms reaching for my embrace
I welcomed the compliments of all who praised you

you have grown tall   strong   independent
you have separated into a man I am proud of

I hide what it costs to let you go
wanting your future to call you forward

Seductions at the Louvre

maybe you need courage   daring   foolishness
to say something to this stranger
everything works against it
routine's nailed you tight
you turn   turn on the wheel of the week
you've compromised with fate
it's easier to go on as before   as before

such desires do not out-last being ignored
the impulse fades   fails to surface
he stays separate   slips further away

safety is sameness   no threats   no changes
no restless nights   no day-dreams
no Apollo as Rilke saw him at the Louvre
balancing on a ball of light
causing him to reflect:
"I must change my life"
no Venus de Milo turning on her pedestal
no glance from *La Gioconda* on a summer afternoon

no "apparition" breaking the shell of the senses
bathing the soul with the beautiful

As if a Façade

(after reading Baudelaire's *Les Fleurs du Mal*)

in the beginning as fevered as Mozart
poetry and love a close knit fabric
while Mozart made love an exquisite lightness
saving every ounce of passion for his music
your scarlet wings carried you into a woman's arms
your trust turned to cinders   your intensity to disgust

innocence and idealism   delicately woven
fine lace breaking when taut
tender odes to beggar women
you clothed their sun-burned skin in blue silk
you bound their coarse hair in white velvet
you placed on their worn feet black satin slippers

you trusted every woman equally
never dreaming   beauty might be a façade
you leap at the archetype
you can't refuse her brown breasts
her serpentine legs and inviting hips
you need to kiss her full lips
bury your face in the aroma of her hair
you can't stop staring into her opal eyes

she refuses her soul to slake your thirst
her arms imprison you   her guiles a trap
her words as ropes to tether you to her bed
bitterness seeds your later work   mocking love
anger injures with a bite   slap   or worse
the residue of early passion in songs for beggar girls
you curse reality   your honesty as courage
is ashes   your last wish   to be transformed

Collaboration Between the Sexes

(Simone de Beauvoir and Jean-Paul Sartre)

was it at the Medici Fountain shaded by plane trees or near the cupids
with pink geranium vases on the terrace overlooking the Luxembourg Gardens
that Simone de Beauvoir met Sartre after classes at the Sorbonne
for conversations about art   the human situation   politics   people
without boredom   wanting the warm weather to last for staying outdoors
and how their young bodies relentlessly climbed mountains of the mind
as in summer they hiked France   Greece   Switzerland   Italy
commenting on particular theses   as if lines in the land   leading this way
or that   stopping in ravines or down unknown terrains of thought
pointing to a remote rampart   an ancient cave or a new promontory
exploring together   then taking a break at a roadside inn or village café
where their wit revived with good wine   an espresso or a shot of whiskey
mixing fun with profundity   poetry   and a little profanity
sometimes losing their balance   high on an idea or deep in confusion
as when in the Alps on their bicycles   plunging headlong into a fall
nearly losing their lives by daring to ride the edge too fast
rescuing each other when necessary from deceptions
from false premises   from posing   from mannered talk   from untruths
as they traveled back roads in strange places where nothing was familiar
except the persistent push to continue as far as possible on a new path
then returning to work in separate apartments in Paris
with endless discussions at Aux Deux-Magots or Le Flore
relaxing at night with Mozart's *Così Fan Tutte*
or catching an American movie or resting at a house in the country
then returning to conversations   readings   writings   political involvements
overcoming storms inherent in new relationships   accepting the pain
but never breaking the vital soul of their friendship

After Reading a Prose Poem by Mallarmé

("The White Water Lily," 1885)

it is you in the rowboat who hides behind thick wild bushes
is it from shyness or from a sustained delight in pretending I am
the woman who has waited for your approach   that I hesitate and invite
your glances   aware of the intricacies of your silent loving
an enchantment mutually held as I study your strong arms
in white rolled back sleeves as you bend   stretch   pull the oars
in a rhythm a man instinctually knows as when he leads a woman
round a dance floor   with care   strength   attention   delight
how in his arms and hands she trusts   sensitivity and pleasure
is it similar   now   with my silhouette as I stroll this park
is entertainment a hidden treasure   a surfacing space   in and out
shadow and light   heather and mulberry   wheat and iris
as I respect your distance yet am not deceived into believing
this fascination is one-sided   when you hear my steps draw closer
as you see my silk dress tremble in anticipation of your nearness
as the details of face   hands   eyes move close as I cross
the small bridge near bouqueted water lilies and glimpse
your struggle to release the allurement   how loosen the white
pink attraction   how subdue your passion for freedom
your strain for privacy   the same known in my breast
I pivot round and wonder if you follow while you hold back
until I hear your oars   ripple   descend   glide   plunge   cross
the smooth surface   you stir the lily's regard   you exit
the enclosure   will you glance back at the bridge   the untouched lily
petals shudder   cry for regard   a paroxysm peculiar to woman
I turn uncertain   is my image intact inside your composure

The Roman Baths, Cathédral St. Sauveur, Aix-en-Provence

I
the tanned   muscular Romans
        harnessed these waters
under plane trees they imagined home
        calling   *veni   veni*

II
the baths border a middle class motel
        decorated by unkempt rose bushes
abandoned lawn chairs   a low chain-link fence
        a high grey wall   peeling plaster   wild ivy
a busy street sending traffic in a loop
        a moss fan in the middle of Cours Mirabeau
a blanket   gathers drip by drip   the basin waits
        café tables   cars coasting past
the "Roman wall" curves north for barren suburbs

III
August blinds with memories of the South
        after two nights' sentry duty the soldier is dizzy
he drenches his black hair in a basin
        he leans against the cloister   closing his eyes
he hears footsteps   smells musk and clover
        she nears the wisteria within his reach
she rushes into Saint Sauveur

IV
he removes his leather and brass shield
     unclasps his breastplate   unfastens his sword
his helmet on the floor   he slips off his sandals
     barefoot on the damp grey granite
(as Saint Louis for his coronation in Notre Dame)
     he sheathes grace in his white tunic
she knows he's strong enough to lift her
     his breath beside her   she forgets
he is the occupier   her heart contracts
     he forgets she is the one conquered
he hesitates in shyness   she encourages
     freely they explore each other

Provençal Summer

I am the see-through blue-green water at the mouth of the Rhone
you are the man who swims home   the one who sailed the white flag-ship
on the liquid dream surfaces   I am the summer coast of your return
night with muslin sheets pulled down at our ankles
reserved words at dinner   we waited   for the afterwards
the moth and mosquitoes on the other side of the screen
the hotel room in a remote corner of Provence   without a phone
your breath in my ear   your warmth over me   my memory fertile
the river banks swelled with electric rains   your skin tasted of sea-salt
at midnight a bird's liquid notes   a messenger of the gods
        Gabriel   Cupid   Apollo
you played in the lilac and lime leaves   I touched your pale blue feathers
your silver breast band caught the sun   the sea and river converged
fresh scented   aquamarine waters pulsed against the shore

Coast of the Saintes Maries, Provence

Provençal   Saintes Maries   pure white shore
    aquamarine water   outside Arles   pearl silk fog
she strips off her blouse for a tan
    while her daughter displays a firm figure
in and out the surf   while she wonders if
    desire sleeps under the skin   if
vulnerability surfaces   shivering in exposure

strolling for the water   distracting the tension
    increasing it as she swims the breast stroke
needing courage to emerge dripping wet
    salt drops streaming on her skin
she opens to his stare   concentrating
    so she can't ignore the pulse
setting her cheeks aflame   that is why
    she pulls on a t-shirt   trying to hide
in the blanket while he persists
    achieving his purpose   a flush rushes
through   she cannot move a muscle   only lie
    on the warm sand   suspended   stunned   tensed
while the young woman jumps up to play volley ball

A French Landscape

wet air on relaxed limbs   the heavy air of hay stacks
train smoke curls at the mountain's waist
underground waters swell in lakes and rivers
a yellow patch-work dress fades at the forest border
a pale moon complexion   morning moisture upon breasts
every muscle of the valley's womb   rhythmed
hair every which-way   braided oak   thick willow   poplar strands
the breeze as a pulse   animals feeding in a wheat field
a mother resting in the shade opening her blouse to her child
a young man noticing the sway of a young woman's hips

a middle aged woman wiping her forehead
with the handkerchief her lover gave before he went away
a husband pausing in pruning his vineyard
remembering the scent of the wedding chamber
the sun's intimate caress   the exhaustion of heat
the western ridge lifting its lips for a final kiss
light resists leaving   clouds   shadow   fog   blanket the valley
night's privacy   the sounds and movements of love
the repeated rituals   remaking day in the dark
soon   the soft breasts of sleep

These Pink Flowers

these pink flowers in September
on the thin lines of branches have a name
I have never learned

as a child they were the only flowers
in our tiny yard in Brooklyn
hanging over the sidewalk

now they bloom in the abundance of California
near honey-suckle   acacias   lemon blossoms
not far from the roses

still their name remains anonymous
having the look of a long journey
having come from afar
now greeting the last bees of an Indian summer
they follow each other on these bushes
        deep purple centers   pale yellow stamens
        orchid pink the five petals blowing

they are the shaded shadows from childhood
        the longing to live in the country
        dreams of a house with windows lighting a front lawn
        images of my father tending a garden
scenes which never would happen

these flowers finish the summer
wind into pale violet strands that sleep in the ground
soon after winter new blossoms come
carrying something unnamed in them

Rouen Cathedral After the War

PRELUDE
I was broken   a folded small creature
my wings spread in the face of a storm
I was brought down and fell on earth
hope trembled in my soul . . .

I

the cathedral in white ash
her glory suppressed
her stained glass splintered
her womb violated

she confided her secret
I was stripped of privacy
I lost my shaded refuge
my art crushed by coldness
my vision in shattered glass

I was lovely in the landscape
though formed as vulnerable
my delicate stories opened a new language
my naïve angels   all potential in their tasks
my sculptured women   virginal and maternal
I trusted those who neared my sanctuary

harmony rose   in crevices
my alcoves patient   expectant
my transepts stretched in tenderness
heavy in joy   I released my songs

II

I was unsuspecting
my nave and altar attacked
my soul ripped open
I was brought near death
close to extinction
my flowers scattered
I feared his power

my apse caved in
my glass melted
my roses crumbled on the marble floor
despair cleaved in my pulse
I cried for mercy
and knew violence

III

in time a prophet came
one who cared for beauty
whose art lifted transepts
who birthed winged arches
who offered garments of grace
who helped heal my scars

his indelible mark
dispersed grief
shadows faded under my eyes
my sanctuary illumined
his voice brought back my songs

Mont Saint Michel

I

the curved lipped sand in a twilight haze
the high granite wall holding all in place
the cobbled street turns in and out the 11th century
searchlights scan damp earth for high tide
silence picks up the slightest inflection
distant   primordial   womb-like the pulse
Michael's wings lift off   encircle the tower
evening enchants him through the swallows
an amber band reclines over Normandy
a restless need surfaces in his middle
a cave   an indentation   a recess   a channel
his fate resides within her destiny
first waters brush blue-green ribbons on her brow
his wings scoop the tide   foam in white caps
a tumbling rush   urgent threads at her breast
she rises in moonlight   lifts a resplendent cup
she shapes his liquid night   the tides climax

II

a clear blue sky   a few clouds over the sea
the sand a tanned blanket in low tide
swallows in the tower   gulls flock the Norman coast
a fisherman casts his net across the channel
the sun appeals plainly to earth
with open arms he wishes to encircle her
while a woman dresses the altar in white linen
placing twin candles on either corner
she stands a summer bouquet on blue-grey tiles
she gathers herself as bread and wine with God
she will surrender on the couch of faith and trust
as she glimpses waves flushing the western rampart
tiny ribbons undulate in their nature close to shore
a silvery foam   films of sheer white fabric
powerful tides surrender under a full moon
dreams   nourishment   sacrifice   communion
this fourfold creation   earth   sky   mortals   the divine
she bows in the nave   awaiting their alignment

III

I ask you   Mont Saint Michel to abide with me
a jewel in morning   noon   evening over the sea
sands firm for a ten mile stretch of coast
you have won me   I glimpse you from the train
your blond ramparts   open gate   hymns   sea-birds
shaped by twilight   you rise over thick green marshes

I climb your wet stones near midnight
up wide stairs under Michael's watchful eyes
as he lifts his wand in tune with the tide
coaxing the waters back and forth to shore
while under his tower the organ swells in song
as pilgrims rest in pews within the sanctuary
hands touch hands in peace   Latin on the tongue

the intimate moment approaches as the soul enfolds
the white dove feathers pressed on the breast
his wings beat the air with golden tenderness
within burnished transepts   the arches relax as home
overcoming lightning storms   despair   evil   wars

now altar roses and the Easter candle with lavender letters
the wick smolders   clouds drift off the sea
I kneel on blue grey tiles

IV

I tell you the color of sand in morning is blond   at twilight grey
that the tide is a definite dark line each time
it approaches or leaves land
and the forests of Brittany lend themselves to legend
as also the open fields of Normandy
so little imagination is needed to see knights in metal and mail
carrying red and gold banners   riding black and white horses
beside women with velvet dresses waving in the wind
while south at the sea's mouth   a fisherman casts his net
and the curve of his arm is the same as the shore
as the rampart running around the entire monastery
like lines on the monk's neck after a heavy sleep on one side
or how the sun sets off a woman's face   caressing shadows and rouge
blazing high past the tree line off the knight's shield
inside the fisherman's net   leaving crisscrossed marks on sand
while Archangel Michael on top the church tower
breaks silence with the birds   in time with the galloping horses
below on the beach beating the air with his sword   a tuning fork
held up by belief   architecture   the elements
while under him   in the austere womb of the Norman church
Italian   Spanish   German   English mix with French
as the kiss of peace ties the tourists together
as in the days when Latin ruled
the same word in each throat   felt in the hands   PAX

V

after dinner we walk the south side circling the mount
past restaurants   homes   inns   built one on top the other
to a small stone chapel on the southern ledge
dedicated to Saint Cuthbert   who offers from his edge
the emerald fields of Brittany   diamond studded in the distance
while round the corner a ribboned ocean's about to rush
inch by inch   foot by foot   leaping   seeking land
immense devotion   haunting   halting   kissing France's feet
while men and women run back between quicksand warnings
Archangel Michael sweeps the sky   slipping the sun west
setting the sequence of evening in motion

VI

teach me the repose of your centuries
        that I might bide my time with grace

the blue sky is lit with your granite tower
        your buttresses rise as lances of hope

what was once full   overflowing with worshipers
        is deserted or kept alive by a handful

yet   in the underground passageways
        arches fan and fan in shaded darkness

while I walk alone and hear my footsteps clearly
        until I stop before an open window facing the sea

come to me   I call   oh white dove
        why are you hidden today in the coast clouds

why are you silent   why not sing in the organ
    why stay aloof in the high tower

while I wander in the chamber below   praying your name
    wanting a rendezvous in the cloister garden

oh return to me   touch my arm with your sun   cross my cheek
    I wait for you to unseal all my senses

keep me company soon under these grey western skies
    in the room of my imagination   when loneliness is acute

II *Vision of Chartres*

After the Queen

after the queen died   kings and bearded gods grew boring
the world emptied   dried   purged of grace and charm
we wanted a resurrection and knew only an absence

finally she swelled in the dark begonia a yellow dust
she was folded in the rose   a fluid birch in the wind
a fountained voice   Rouen's bells   twin towered Chartres
a soprano's crescendo tearing every seam of resistance

she contoured hills   creviced valleys for moisture
she flamed the southern shore   flaunting her pleasures
she rushed in foam of waves and sensuous sunflowers

men called her name   opened their arms   fondled her figure
women wore green silk   blue satin   grey wool   white linen
with pearl earrings to market   an heirloom in their cleavage
a brooch of their grandmother pinned over their breast

artists contemplated her strolling the Luxembourg Gardens
they perspired with the wish for possession
she gave music   stories   portraits   sculpture   dances
she offered herself beside the Medici fountain

we named her Marie Thérèse   Anne   Simone   Blanche   Catherine   Éléonore
we housed her as Venus   Niké   Mona Lisa   Diana   the Virgin
she flavored summer afternoons with an unforgettable fever

we kept the rendezvous a secret   she was near   we were her
she was never promiscuous   only passionate and private
she gave her soul to very few

The Virgin of the Annunciation

(Painted stone, Île-de-France, 14th century)

so striking what she tries to hide with a veil and hand on her full breast
leaning sideways as if in shyness with her other arm on the Book of Hours
as pleasure joins intelligence   breaking out in joy
relaxing the curves of her mouth   moving every detail of her body
as she sits off to the side with the folds of her clothes clinging
her heaviness making the cincture round her waist tighter   more alluring
when yesterday she performed her usual routine without thought of change
the pressure of ripeness sweetened her form   the Spirit fell in love with her
as she strolled the garden   making himself irresistible with his words
in the excitement of his coming she sat down on the chair beside the stream
the brush of doves released from their cages in the pine forest
she smiled him a welcome   knowing he headed home to her arms
now her expression's delightful even to the eyes of the 20th century
she seems both chaste and sensual   the way of a woman with God

Annunciation

her room for revelation   space for God
though she never imagined such love adhering to her womb
that the seed would spin as a star into her earth

her way   not silent or passive
but intense   vivacious   active

a woman ready to embrace life
holding intimacy close   shaping details for the first time
with her eyes' color   her subtle hands   her rhythmed walk

the secret grew visible in her body
she couldn't hide it   even if she wanted
feelings concentrated on forming the finest fruit

she gave words the world wanted   rushing in her breast
every line of grace as in a Gothic cathedral
translucent skin   thick hair   reflective eyes   strong arms

for a perfect tiny form   ancient soul of the universe
maturing at her center   she called her son

Notre Dame

you dream his future as you hold him in your arms
without thought of personal ambitions
not realizing his beauty features your face
his charm   intelligence   your grace made man

is this why you're so approachable
empty of self   radiantly close
your hands wings of grace and understanding
you expose in every line   how you love

I scan your ancient residences   Chartres   Reims   Paris
struck by glances   once given   that continually give
a Queen ruling the twin domains of heaven and earth
as you carry in your left arm   on your hip   the infant God

you sit in the garden pavilion   overlooking the lake
he leans back in your lap as your right hand lifts an Anjou pear
he counts berries on a string   pages in the Book of Hours blow back
sparrows sway on a rose bush   red-orange on white

I desire the earth on my lips where you walked
how men and women used to for their king
my wish to press close on the grass where you stood
as your fragrance pierces me   the white dove your breast

Approaching Her

the liquid lace of steeples
thick wet sand finishing off the top
smooth arches   centuries of rubbing
curved space   burnished wood   blond light

winter withdrawing from blue to red
shadowed lids opening
Latin hymns from the body of Spring
cool granite underfoot warming

scent of incense   cleaving clouds
teasing eyes and nose
covering head and shoulders
caressing the breast

the Virgin's life carved in ivory
conception to coronation
imagining the impossible
a woman giving God human form

music mounts the wide sanctuary womb
columned legs stretch   shoulders arch in apses
unveiling the highest jewel of Gothic glory   the spiral conch
revealing the pure color conceived in the heart of the rose

Near Her

tilt back your head to recall
her columns within reach
her windows in your eyes
her spirals in your heart

without a doubt her power
spread wide and thick in apse and nave
firm on her throne
embracing compassion

no room for ridicule at her altars
she's ancient Roman   Frank   Druid
her labyrinth and alcoves pulse with history
birth   passage   death   resurrection

she melts scorn   her words of stone
powerful hands and bosom   hidden sanctuary fire
unexpected motions   earthquake in the psyche
tides of towering feeling   patience of the deep crypt

her solitude's a decided direction
her body shields the soul
she protects Paradise
she magnetizes the veins   eyes   muscles   memory

Inside Chartres

enter Chartres under her north rose door
down granite steps of a half-lit crypt
lamps swinging in a distant labyrinth
an aisle of caned chairs faces a modern altar

a brown-red Madonna with a child in her lap

a sign says:

> "Her eyes are on her Son,
> through Christ the path to God"

imagine the sign saying:

> "She conceals her essence   God's seed   her Sun rising
> as Apollo from the sea   she is container   chalice   origin
> ocean for sky   earth for tree   womb for beginning
> she refuses to raise her head   eyes entirely on Him
> not for dogma   not in fear of the Trinity
> a woman's privilege   no need explaining
> her hands relaxed in ruling
> her hair hidden in a scarf
> her dress conceals her shape
> as vowed in prayer
> as a pregnant woman in repose"

while upstairs over the high altar in a sheltering apse
she shoulders flying buttresses   reveals nude colors
deep blue   thick red   yellow in a French field
Mediterranean green waters washing white beaches
brown expressive eyes   accented arches
the suggestion of a smile

modern minds hesitate   superstition suspected
stay seated in the south side   looking at her north face
the infant God playing on her knees
the relaxed gaze of a summer afternoon
She draws us   even with eyes closed

Chartres

the crypt
concealed deep
within the earth

a carved labyrinth
a weight
secured in large stones

an alcove for an ancient Madonna
with ample body
a heavenly child on her lap

in semi-darkness
male and female voices sing
they light candles of hope

a secret chamber
hid the Virgin's veil
saving the church from fire

I touch the bare stone altar
lean over a dark well
seek her form

a brilliant sun
enlightens
the shaded walls

roses pour
ruby   agate   gold   turquoise   rust
on the floor   altar   on my palms

Ecce Ancilla Domini

the smallest sounds of the heart
birds returning home by radar
wings wiping a wide sky
a decided direction
a voice forming
God drawing closer to woman
a candle in a crypt
in solitude her "yes"
giving the divine a human body
protecting his place near her breast

The Birthing Garment at Chartres

(for Charlotte)

I

behind the main altar   a transparent chemise
        framed by gold   bound in glass   protected by angels
a miraculous kind cloth   hundreds of years old
        this gift of Constantine to Charlemagne
King Philippe bestowed on the people of Chartres
        this solitary flame   no longer touched
how whitely textured   how streaked by age
        a delicate fabric woven for a king's coming

II

this is her first pregnancy
        she weaves divine spirit and human flesh
under her heart the rhythm starts
        the midwife offers confidence
in baths of scented waters
        covering her shoulders with white linen
crossing near her entrance folds
        a filigree flowers   a panting breath
pain absorbs as she grasps the sheets
        bannering God's push forward
through her labyrinth—*Lux aeternum*—
        she wipes the blood from his face
she opens the gauze round her breasts
        his tiny mouth finds her food
Paradise seems restored

III

in California Charlotte weaves white cotton
 a birthing garment folded on a cream silk bed
scarlet puffed gauze at the throat and entrance
 every detail edged in delicate strength

women under a September moon in an adobe courtyard
 Ilse plays the recorder Jo Ann creates a chant
Carol Lee pregnant seven months leads a belly dance
 a nearby woman prays for a fertile womb

IV

Mary of Chartres slips the garment over her head
 the organ releases *"Alleluia Alleluia"*
Regina Pacis Regina Coeli Regina Aeterna
 her terra-cotta figure enthroned on the wall
scepter in hand the infant comforted in her arms
 transparency folded in her foundation at Chartres

The North Window

she is the light of Chartres' winter
warm hands in roots retreating
sap in the pulse of sleep
seed   nut   fruit   flower

walled womb pulling north
snow breath   pine grove
humus of potent roses   gladiolus
an absorbing personal love

protective star on earth's border
jewel on mountain breasts
fir   down   skin   grass   leaves
touched and tasted

central pulse of the compass
embracing north   south   east   west
electricity of hope   no matter the weather
familiar friends   queen   and   companion

whistling through the windows of our soul
pressing up the damp crypt of our ribs
fingertips on lips   petals   altar   apse
sweet aroma   earth   after winter waiting

Belle-Verrière

(The Blue Window, 1180)

how near you are   womanly god
within reach of my arms
angels at your knee
offer incense in gold containers
your large shoulders desire confidences
your broad forehead suggests intelligence
you shelter yourself with a blue cloak
lilies quiver in vases by your feet
your ancient names in fiery incense
Regina Coeli   Maris Stella   Rosa Mystica
your magnificent shaped forest green   burgundy
gold   ethereal blue   every muscle intent on love
roses bloom all year   spin from your soul

At the Side Altar

the vases full of lilies   the incense raised by young arms
few come to her table   few believe she exists

she is remembered vaguely as mother of God
they forget her magnetism   her wisdom

her heart is full of compassion
she nourishes with liquid earth

she is not bound by rigid rules
she is flexible   free and strong

she is kind when ambition rages
her laughter breaks through the clouds

sometimes a man offers her a caressing glance
noticing her noble heart   guessing her name

rose   peace   Eurydice   Psyche   La Gioconda   Queen Marie of Chartres

The Introit

we enter the radiance of Chartres
embraced by the heart of the rose
transparent blue   crushed ruby
agate of all our emotions

queen of the sun's temple
touching the skin of clouds
sleeping on the moon's pillow
tender in the language of night

queen on an ancient throne
concealing privacy
curtaining strength
counseling men and women

enjoying jokes   acrobats   dances
relieving anxieties
as the child on her lap
lifts his lips to her breast

her handprint in windows
her liquid light through glass
her blood in the white doved Spirit
she is the way in and out

78

Kyrie

mother   sister   *regina*
compassionate home
womb of origin

private space
where love is conceived
fruit of Wisdom in woman

lucid life of this people and place
pregnant field   heavy and fair
wheat   poppy   sunflower   poplar

flamed feathers from shoulders
brown sheaves in your arms
black haired   dark eyed

strong   sensual   subtle   scented
your palm print on every hour
exquisitely expressed

rosed glass   ivory storied
promise on the sky-line
meaning mercy and love

Confiteor

lift our guilt to your lips
in your embrace we confess
fear   and   selfishness

you are the balm on our wounds
the lily scented in water
the fur of the rose

you open the doors
you bind hurts and set the broken strong
you bring tenderness back into the proud

you hold in your cupped hands
water that refreshes
milk   and the wine of love

oh sacred place on this earth
we touch your tenderness   kiss your crypt
kneel in your power without embarrassment

you make it easy to say we are sorry
you are the push of each beginning
you are the rest at the end of effort

we contemplate our finiteness
your gaze blesses and frees our soul
you place passion in our being again

The Gloria

glory   glorious   gorgeous rose
multicolored medallion
Notre Dame de Chartres

patient protection
bosomed flower
natural no   generous yes

bud   dream   blueprint
ancient memory   towering ages
essence unerased

bursting brilliance containing all color
private powerful pulse of love
glory   glorious   gorgeous rose

Credo

I believe in your Gothic contours   towering over blond wheat
over seven hundred years as sentinel for Chartres
rising from the history of the unconscious
rejected   repressed   in prison
secretly loved for centuries
pushed to the edge of belief

I hesitate in expectation
as on the plane from America   as on the train from Paris
winding north-west   a long tunnel   a station   a small park
an uphill walk   finally finding you at the end of the street
granite foundation   sun-lit door   broad buttresses

I enter your court   temple   cathedral
green   red   purple   blue   gold
you unveil and conceal the sweet face of God
seldom seen   shadowed   rosed complexion
your crypt contains a secret well

I believe you are God's feminine country
balancing rule with laughter   teaching with song
I believe you are the ancient holy ground
rising walls   proud shy breasts   intimate   vulnerable   nurturing
a sign between French fields   over the city rampart   in our soul

I believe you are conscious of your power
waiting for a rendezvous with science
for the genes of the psyche to gravitate home
as the Crusaders after their obsessions of the Middle Ages
returning to woman's courts of love

I believe you grasp us to your heart every hour
as the Angelus   day and night   dips into dreams
bringing us back to places as Chartres
before your nave to gaze at your rosed compassion
sunlit   transparent   with doves diving in your breast

I believe you return as Eurydice to Orpheus
not sinking back to the underworld
but embracing Orpheus for daring to look
for the courage to call her name
to reach for her hand
I believe you are the eternal woman

Sanctus

holy   holy   holy
holy mother   holy other
holy   holy   One

nearest sister
dearest daughter
beloved One

container   chalice   liquid food
essential womb   inviting home
holy   holy   holy   One

sweet steeples
soaring songs   sequential seasons
holy hands healing

incense   musk   jasmine
haven and holder of God
holy temple   hold us

84

Consecration

long ago she walked earth
mounted these stairs to her throne
and said

I give myself
as a woman who leaves distractions aside
every muscle moving with the heart's blood

I remember you
in privacy as a woman gathers life
in her arms   around her womb

you say my name publicly as the rose is named
jewel on my Queen's heart
blazing over wheat fields
moving in veins   muscles   emotions

so when drinking milk or wine
when seeing your monthly blood
when touching with love

remember this is my body   blood   spirit
food for the world
as in the beginning   now   and always

The Canon

you are the woman who wove in your womb
the love of the Holy Spirit
who preceded other women
with your powerful "yes"
forming his body and soul
signing such an ethereal sound as God
into the singular human form of a child

you promise possibility
hands over your womb
over home   city   country   the world
where privacy is protected
where the fruit is small   large   sacred   secular
profound   casual   serious   shadowed   shining

you redeem failures   disappointments
rescuing all from oblivion
your yes heads the procession
trumpet   organ   violin   song
banners fly blue   green   yellow   mauve
dancers in the aisle   children on your lap
ordinary people carry dreams in their bodies   to your altar

Kiss of Peace

your kiss lasts a lifetime
keeps going on

you embrace the dark of sunflower
the veiled winter   the core of the lily

you stand windowed   rose colored
shadowed in curving side altars

your kiss is essentially   everything tender and strong
your vessels perfume the Gothic conch

we kiss your holy place
you wish us peace

Agnus Dei

lamb of God protect us from the cold
shed your coat to clothe us
gentle   strong   resilience
leaping over dark crevices
permanent home over the town of Chartres
you want to touch and be touched
goodness without naiveté
wisdom born of storms
strength and surrender
God's golden fleece and ours
you are at peace at the heart of the rose

Communion

your lap and breast as home   altar worn by kisses
ancient face shaped by anonymous hands in terra-cotta

your crypt understands every longing
holding in darkness at your well   labyrinth   altar

arms round our shoulders   knighted for victory by your strength
place of power   hundreds of years old and new each century

rose walled Chartres over the garden   town   country   world
waiting for rain   light   for man and woman's touch

you mix the four seasons in our bloodstream
the moon's cycles   returning tides   moods   rotation   axis

our vow to you is the praise of cathedral arches
curving in graceful granite gestures   so no war will destroy

your enormous heights   your private foundation
your beloved being   shapes surprises

your doubled doors allow communion in our hands   on our tongue
your cave the rosed apse's light   embedded as a broach on the breast

A Litany

hail tower of ivory   intense white
hail *rosa mystica*   without hurting thorns
hail *regina coelorum*   hail earthly delight
hail temple of God   sweet incense   oil   musk

hail virgin   sister   lover   mother   wisdom
you give as gardens   where deer graze   birds fly in loops
where mimosa   birch   willow   thrive and privacy is a green hedge
a lake where turtles turn over in pleasure
a garden not lost   not needing reform or to be refound

hail symbol and signifier   whose palms praise earth
whose breastbone   breath   rise and fall with love
whose pain and brilliancy births hope
who nurtures in a time of nuclear threat
who prepares a first and future home

yours the skills and grace of prayer   protection   notation
hieroglyphics   healing   painting   cooking   imagining
yours the flower   lips   forest   lines   container   slope
cup   silk   circulation   seat   curves   center   silence   children

you make summer heavy leaved   autumn a reluctant attachment
Spring is slow motion in your fingers   uncurling the sweet-gum tree
your perspiration on our forehead   or winter's sap concentrated
as a woman teaches   dances   paints   designs   mothers   ministers

you erase mirages of want-ads that hint at easy sex
you dismiss fetishes of women devouring men
you dress or undress before the mirror
yours the permission or not   man standing at the door

your body is fragranced   flowered   pearled   feathered
hail milk skin   amber   brown   black   womaned earth
we hail your neck   shoulders   heart region   privacy   soul
canvas   music   word   photo   dance   pregnancy utterance

hail eternal essence unfolding as we enfold
your sounds shape Eden's entrance and exit
your twin towers of compassion and pleasure
wounds and ecstasies   welcoming   amen   *alleluia*

Adieu Chartres

it is at the back of Chartres where her buttresses
cast her towers into the sky
there her strength is recognized
and felt by the eyes and even by touch
as we sit on the bench under an elm tree
overlooking the city's roofs   complex shapes   and chatter comes
from homes   schools   shops   parks   cafés   cars   buses
as people join together to work   play   or make love
so we lean along the ledge running round the eastern side
over thick green terraces of ancient gardens   burial grounds
holding hands   vibrating with the organed heart
with the church behind us   steaming with incense and candles
cooling off continually from her underground crypt
whose mixture is a shaded   contained warmth
making the landscape contemplative and impassioned
inside and out the cathedral   so what we see
moves in our pulse   the blond wheat   rimmed poplars
expansive horizon   a league   a secrecy
a rose lifting its body in our breast
as with all great loves   exhausting   haunting
afterwards   reminding us what was shared
promising more   if we return . . .

III *Gestures of the Word*

Advent

I

the finale of summer is always December
when the pines of our Santa Cruz range
keep us company with multicolored ornaments of hope
while far in the south is our relinquished warmth
what shortened days remind us of—

the lazy August repose on white heated sand
the grove of pelicans that skimmed high tide
the tourists sauntering along Capitola's Main Street

now is the season we seek for remembrance
as the caravans once crossed the Sierras—
we will not be deferred from dreams
nor erase a clear winter's light
nor still the breath or incense of desire
for the one waited for   the one who comes

II

in the open doorway
a brilliant winged messenger
unfolds his strong hand
where a lily blossoms

his words are
not without pain
"yes" must be generous
not a guaranteed contentment

it is necessary
for the poppies
to dip underground in shadow
if to rise as flamed tongues in summer

come   said the angel
come   store the sap
learn how the invisible
works without worry

each month his nearness
shapes the enfolded secret
under her heart
the ripening Word

My Muse

ah artful companion
anonymous in fate
no less lovely my angel
is your heavy woven hair

full bodied lips
arching brow
irresistible song
furrowed eyes

my home near your breast
quiet in afternoon shade and light
as the organ swells in song
roses tumble   wine colored to earth

through you I offer myself again
to the inexhaustible One
whose composure grounds
my passion in his presence

Annunciation

grace goes to you
the dove dives down
his white feathers and scarlet throat
brings God's breath close
between opening folds
finds your life

your purple cloth divides
you unclasp the pearl
kiss the unexpected
invite the voice of angel
making room for him
in your expectant self

you speak words
clearer than in a letter
your essential "yes"—
who else loves like this—
you make God's word
flesh and blood

"yes"   you say   "yes"
your body and soul
a womanly embrace
entirely given over . . .
you make love
you shape love

In the Forest

(after Franz Marc's *The Doe*)

she fell as a doe   with sudden grace collapsed
she touched her heart   felt the arrow
the blood of herself all over the grass

she lay on a private path in the shelter of hawthorn
where high pines and oaks wave against blue reaches of heaven
where patches of sunlight move the shade

her art lay exhausted beside her
she stroked it as a mother does a sick child
a gesture at reassurance
when doubt and death tear at the breast

the words she gave him   cried for regard
they knocked on her womb
her memory keen in its art knew
every inflection that needed saving

for a long time she lay delirious
breathing with difficulty
the pale pink sweater worn for his pleasure
lay beside her   stained by blood

he left   knowing she was wounded
he went about his work
visited friends
kept himself untouched by the personal

he left her for dead
she would try and save herself
coax back her art with gentle words
resurrect the gardens of France

she will read beloved authors
resay their words in her heart
she wants more than survival
she wants to sing again

With the Oil of Myself

with the oil of myself
vesseled   I carry faithfulness
to the outskirts of the city

I am a woman my religion disowns
never again will there be a home for me
in their house of worship

I am a pilgrim searching
for the Holy Grail in a modern form
the intimate shape of God

if my eyes glow
it is with the light
of his regard
the kiss of his return

I will not be one
who rests in the company of crowds
neither will I be comfortable
in releasing my art for analysis

in the slow accretion of time
I embrace the child in a white dress
who held the sacred candle
and knew the sanctuary's incense
for his advent

where is he now you ask me
few words are capable of containing him
yet he is nearer   closer than my skin
within my left hand   under my palm
over my heart-pulse   his heaviness

I tremble as Lawrence in that flash
of spirit infleshed   when tears mix
with music   flooding our senses
near as self or nearer

elusive cadences rise
out of nothingness
they take a human form
and wish clothing for words

Gestures of the Word

you rode a white horse between pines   high
on the horizon   your figure drew me   I listened
as you stepped on the stones and touched my arm
saying my name   for the first time with undisguised emotion
I shivered under your gaze and lost my train of thought
I laughed as your expressions leaped   somersaulted   spun
you lit off firecrackers   twisting   tickling phrases
as a Balzac   your words teased   startled   wrapped round me
as a Mozart in exquisite metaphors   flowering at every angle
a strip of sun scorched my eyes   your gorgeous music gathered
swift   powerful   mellow   secret   incomparable   at last
patience yielded a singular flower   golden-mauve
a landscape changed by language   scented adjectives
bronze verbs   gold convictions   shaded conflicts
turquoise longing   as each other's audience   we laughed
dancing with words   skipping across the lake's surface
in couched innuendos   you rowed a scarlet winged ship
I flew blue banners from the château's façade   your speech
raided   a turret   a chimney   a chapel   a tower   a golden bell
a cabinet of burnished oak   opening treasures of golden prose
a terrain vibrating from Cupid's arched bow   you carried me
beyond the architect's original intention   tuned to heights
underground caverns   harmonized widths   shapely arches
against a buoyant horizon   your light eyes flashed
I cried for their glory   as the spring leapt from the south
side of the forest into a fountained pulse   rushing through
channeled sounds   a scented bouquet   as words kissed
we broke free as a wild horse across the lawn

my breathless shyness still   I threw aside reserve
joining my words to yours   we touched every inch of the senses
without needing to touch   igniting the earth under us   scorching
lines in the landscape   leaving an incision on the soul

Solitude

it is how a woman waits
in the enveloping light of afternoon
drying her hair by the window
her shoulders inclined slightly forward
so her strong arms and legs suggest
concealment as well as invitation

I am learning the value of repose
for you have blessed my solitude
in the Louvre I see your mark in numerous paintings
as you protect the secrecy of woman
and understand her prayer and desire

that is why in the sanctuary of solitude
in the silence before the words
in the waiting that is truly free
in the concentration before the piano keys are touched
in the memory of beloved rooms   galleries   forests
gardens   rivers   bays   and blank pages
there is no longer loneliness
but the completion that is grace
when solitude effuses a fragrant communion
for those visited by love

Thérèse of Lisieux

all the love you carried for God
ripened as a rose in your body
your lips parted   you sang with power
as a Tosca   when desire is seamless
and prayer takes on a womanly form
with memory as a guide over his words
or in morning   in the cloister garden
as blond pillars enfolded white myrtle buds
the fountain lay open to the sun
you came with his words in your hands
the pages blazed between the cover
vulnerable in their loveliness
you touched his essence as you read
God lived secretly in sounds
with gold white wings
with a scarlet throat whose voice was lightning
as at the Annunciation when the dove circled Mary
and she saw the gold band round his brow
while you   dressed in convent clothes
lived for moments of contemplation
as his language   sunk in you   would rise
near as breath   intimate as your pulse
within the cloister garden's delicate fluting
fragrant roses   dripping water   lilies of the valley
under the olive tree   you coaxed his return
named him in prayer on your tongue
at home in your breast